The Gleamings Guidebook to Writing Your Life Story

Janice Lane Palko

The Gleamings Guidebook to Writing Your Life Story

ISBN: 978-0-9984296-0-1

CONTENTS

Why You Should Write Your Life Story

Congratulations! You have taken the first step to completing your or your loved one's life story.

Several years ago, I began working as a freelance writer, interviewing subjects and writing articles for a magazine. After interviewing subjects from the Lt. Governor of Pennsylvania, to decorated war heroes, to average citizens, I realized something: Not only is the title of the song "Every Picture Tells a Story," true, but also every life tells a story.

Sadly, I also realized that too many of these stories are never preserved. In my own life, precious histories have been lost forever with the passing of loved ones.

My great-grandmother often told me a tale of how, when she was a small child at the beginning of the past century, she traveled by covered wagon from Pittsburgh, Pennsylvania, to Steamboat Springs, Colorado. She recounted her adventure to me when I was a little girl, but unfortunately, time has dimmed my memory, and I can't recall any of the details or the reason why her family embarked on such a journey.

When she died, not only did I lose her, but her life history as well. Wanting to prevent others from experiencing such a loss, I founded Gleamings Personal Historian Services. I have taught classes about writing life histories and have ghostwritten memoirs to help students and clients remember the times of their lives and then preserve them in a tangible manner.

Thomas Carlyle said, “Life is a gleaming between two eternities.”

Gleamings Personal Historian Services was founded on the belief that no two people, no two lives, are ever the same and that your unique spark of life, your gleaming, should be preserved before it is extinguished and lost forever.

To help you write your or your loved one’s personal history, I’ve compiled the questions I developed and have used when interviewing clients and have published them in this easy-to-use guidebook.

Once again, congratulations for undertaking such a worthwhile project. Now, turn the page and prepare to have the time of your life!

How to Use This Guidebook

This guidebook of questions is your key to unlocking your past and preserving your personal history. There are many options for recording your life story, but no matter which method you choose, it all begins with drawing out memories. These questions encompass every phase of life and will help you to write a comprehensive memoir.

The questions are arranged chronologically from birth to later life and are grouped by life stages. Most of the questions will pertain to you or the person you are interviewing. Some will not. You may answer as many or as few as you want. This is your life to record it as you please.

A Memory Refresher Guide has been included. Before beginning, it is advisable to review the items listed there to refresh the memory. Keep a notebook and pen on hand while you peruse these items so that you can note names and dates and any memories that spring to mind that you want to be sure to include in your personal history. This is also a good opportunity to select photographs and documents you would like to include in your memoir.

After reviewing these items, it's wise to decide the manner in which you wish to preserve your history. There are many options. The simplest way to preserve your memories is with good old paper and pen. There is nothing wrong with penning your own story. What a treasure it would be to have a handwritten history!

There are several cautions to keep in mind, however, when producing a handwritten life story. Make sure your paper is acid free and use ink that will not fade with time. Also, if doing a handwritten personal history, make sure you have legible penmanship. Imagine how frustrating it would be for your descendants to have a keepsake that is deteriorating or illegible.

Another simple way is to dictate the answers to the questions into a recorder, or if you are more technologically inclined, videotaping your replies is a method to consider.

The most common way to preserve your memories is in book form. With the ease of using computer word processing programs, composing, formatting, and printing your life story has never been easier.

Printing and binding options are numerous and range from inexpensive to heirloom quality. For those on a budget, printing your personal history using a desktop printer and preserving the manuscript in a binder is an economical solution. For those wanting a professional quality work, visit your local copy center, where binding options from coil, tape, or perfect bindings are available. They can also help with layout and design. For hardcover personal history books, consult your phone directory for local bookbinders. Another option is to self-publish your memoir through an online publisher such as CreateSpace. There are numerous books on self-publishing that can guide you through that process—and possibly, if you are so inclined, to sell your memoir.

No matter what option you choose, your personal history will be a treasure you and your descendants will cherish!

Some Considerations . . .

Often when beginning a personal history, issues arise. The most common is: What if I don't remember? Unfortunately, memories fade with time, and as you recall aspects of your life, you or your subject may be a bit foggy on the details. It's perfectly acceptable to add phrases like, "As best as I recall," or "My recollection is a bit hazy, but this is what I remember," etc.

Another issue that arises is about honesty. How honest should you be? The objective of writing a personal history is not only to preserve your memories, but also to enable your readers to gain an understanding of who you are.

Therefore, you should tell as much about yourself as you feel comfortable, keeping in mind your audience. Your great-grandchildren don't need nor would they appreciate a detailed description of your wedding night.

On the other hand, no life escapes hardship, tragedy, mistakes, or suffering. Events such as these shape people—sometimes more so than life's joyous moments. These types of sensitive memories, should you wish to include them—and you are under no obligation to do so—can be written about tactfully and in such as manner that you can tell the story and how it affected you, but without being too graphic.

When writing a life story, often the concern arises as to how to treat someone who has mistreated you. Certainly, if there has been an unpleasant episode that is important to you or your subject's life history, it should be included. However, instead of dwelling on the wrong, a more positive way to handle this dilemma is to highlight how you dealt with this adversity. It will paint you in a more favorable light. In general, avoid bashing another in print. It will only reflect poorly on you.

No matter the memory or the subject, one rule to keep in mind above all others is: Once something is in print, it can't be taken back.

Now turn the page and begin your life story.

Memory Refresher Guide

Before beginning your personal history it's beneficial to prepare by refreshing your memory or the memory of the subject you plan to interview. Below is a list of items you may want to examine. While you are reviewing these artifacts, it's also helpful to make notes of any memory that springs to mind that you want to be sure to include in your life story.

Enjoy your trip down Memory Lane!

Photo Albums/Home Movies/Videos - (This is also a good time to select treasured photos and any documents you may want to include in your story.)

Documents – Birth certificates, baptismal certificates, marriage licenses, medical records, death certificates, burial plot information.

Heirlooms/Keepsakes – Letters, postcards, report cards, greeting cards, programs, ticket stubs, etc.

Scrapbooks/Yearbooks

Baby Books/Immunization Records

Diaries/Journals

Legal Documents – Wills, deeds, adoption decrees, divorce papers, immigration papers, etc.

Military Records – Discharge papers, medals, commendations, etc.

Recipes – (You may choose to include in your story one or two family recipes or home remedies.)

Family Trees or Genealogy Information

Family Bible

Questionnaire-1

Family History, Birth, and Preschool Years

1. What is your date of birth?

2. Where were you born? State? Country? Hospital? At home?

3. Do you know how much you weighed or the time you were born?

4. Any unusual circumstances about your birth or your mother's pregnancy? (If you were adopted, you may also complete Questionnaire 2.)

5. What is your mother's name (including maiden name)? Do you know her birth date? Where she was born? Where she grew up?

6. Who were her parents? Names? Birth dates? Where were they born? Death dates and cause of death? Can you tell something you remember about each of them?

7. What do you remember about her family? Did she have brothers and sisters? Their names? Birth dates? Death dates? Can you tell something you remember about each of them?

8. What did your mother look like? What did her family look like?

9. What kind of people were they? Their personality? Their heritage?

10. Did they observe any special traditions? Holidays? Have any special skills? Make special foods? Belong to a religion?

11. How much education did your mother receive? Where did she attend school?

12. Did she have an occupation? If so, name all the places where she worked.

13. If deceased, when did she die? What caused her death? How did her passing affect you?

14. What do remember most about your mother?

15. What is your father's name? Do you know his birth date? Where he was born? Where did he grow up?

16. Who were his parents? Names? Birth dates? Where were they born? Death dates and cause of death? Can you tell something that you remember about each of them?

17. What do you remember about his family? Did he have brothers and sisters? Names? Birth dates? Death dates? Can you tell something that you remember about each of them?

18. What did your father look like? What did his family look like?

19. What kind of people were they? Their personality? Their heritage?

20. Did they observe any special traditions? Holidays? Have any special skills? Make special foods? Belong to a religion?

21. How much education did your father receive? Where did he attend school?

22. Did he have an occupation? If so, name all the places where he worked.

23. If deceased, when did he die? What caused his death? How did his passing affect you?

24. What do you remember most about your father?

25. Do you look like your mother or father? Was your personality like theirs at all or were you very different from them?

26. How did your parents meet? How long did they date?

27. When did they marry? Where did they marry? Did they take a honeymoon? If so, where?

28. Where did they live when first married?

29. How did they support themselves?

30. Do you have any sisters? If so, their names and birth dates?

31. Do you have any brothers? If so, their names and birth dates?

32. What is your birth order? (Oldest child, middle, baby, etc.)

33. Did you enjoy your order of birth?

34. Can you tell something about each of your siblings?

35. Were you closer to any of your siblings?

36. What is your first memory? Describe it in detail.

37. Do you know if you had an attachment to a favorite blanket, toy, pacifier, etc.? What became of this comfort item?

38. Did you have any childhood fears? How did you overcome them?

39. Did you have any pets?

40. Did you have a nickname? If so, how did you acquire it?

41. Did you have any bad habits or problem behaviors as a child? Nail biting, bedwetting, temper tantrums, etc. How did you overcome this behavior?

42. Can you describe in detail the holidays your family observed and how they were celebrated?

43. What is the most memorable holiday you remember?

44. What was the house like that you lived in as a child? Where was it located? Can you describe it inside and outside?

45. Can you describe your room? Did you share a room with anyone?

46. How long did you live there?

47. Did you have any chores around the house? How did you feel about your tasks?

48. Did you ever move from this home? If so, how many times did you move? To where? And when? And how long did you live at each place? Can you describe each home?

49. Did you have any childhood illnesses? Operations? What kind of medical treatment did you receive?

50. Did you have any favorite toys? Games? Stories? Nursery Rhymes? Songs? Heroes?

51. Who were your playmates?

52. Any favorite foods or foods you absolutely hated?

53. Did you travel or go on any family vacations?

54. Were you breast or bottle fed?

55. Any memorable experiences you want to include?

Questionnaire-2

Adoption

(If you were not adopted, please skip to Questionnaire 3.)

1. When did you find out that you were adopted?

2. How did you come to learn that you were adopted?

3. How did you feel when you found out that you were adopted?

4. What do you know of your birth mother, if anything?

5. What do you know of your birth father, if anything?

6. Do you know if you have any biological siblings?

7. What do you know about the circumstances of your birth? Where were you born?

8. What do you know of the circumstances of your adoption?

9. How old were you when your adoptive parents received you?

10. Was your name changed when you were adopted?

11. Have you made contact with any members of your birth family?

12. If you did, how was that experience?

13. If you haven't made contact with your birth family, was there a reason?

14. If you made contact with your birth family, how did your adoptive parents feel about your doing so?

15. How do you feel about your birth mother?

16. How do you feel about your birth father?

17. What do you know of your biological family's medical history?

18. Do you feel a person is more influenced by their biological heritage or by the environment in which they are raised?

19. In general, how do you feel about adoption?

20. What insights would you share with someone who is adopted?

21. What insights would you share with someone who is considering adopting a child?

Questionnaire-3

School Days

1. When did you enter school?

2. Were you excited to enter school?

3. What school did you attend? Where was it located?

4. What type of school was it? Private? Parochial? Public?

5. Can you describe your school building? Your classroom?

6. What grade did you start with?

7. Do you remember what you wore on your first day?

8. What were your feelings on your first day?

9. How did you get to school? How far away was it from home?

10. How many students were in your class? In the school?

11. What was your principal's name?

12. Who was your first teacher? What was he/she like? Did you like him/her?

13. What was a typical school day like?

14. What kind of supplies did you have? What kind of books?

15. Who were your school friends?

16. What did you do for lunch? What did you usually eat?

17. What did you do at recess?

18. What subjects did you like best? The least?

19. What did children wear to school then? What kind of hairstyles?

20. How many years did you attend this school?

21. How was discipline handled in your school?

22. Were you ever in trouble? Were you ever sent to the principal's office? If so, why?

23. Can you remember the name of the teacher for each grade that you attended school?

24. What kind of grades did you achieve?

25. Do you remember how holidays were celebrated in school?

26. Did you participate in any activities, sports, programs? Play an instrument?

27. Did your school have a team nickname or school colors?

28. If you left school early, in what grade did you leave? What was the main reason?

29. What was the name of the first book you ever read?

30. Did you receive any awards or honors in school?

31. As a child, what did you want to be when you grew up?

32. Any other memory that you can recall from your early school years?

Questionnaire-4

Teen and High School Years

1. Did your family celebrate birthdays?

2. If so, how did they celebrate them? Do you remember any gifts that you received?

3. Did you have any special birthday celebrations? Sweet Sixteen, etc.?

4. How did you feel about becoming a teenager?

5. Was more expected from you as you grew older? Were you awarded more privileges?

6. What type of teenager were you? Rebellious? Carefree? Sullen? Typical?

7. If you went to high school, what was the name of the school?

8. What was your high school building like? Where was it located?

9. How many students attended your high school?

10. What was your school's nickname? Alma Mater? School colors?

11. How did you get to school? How long did it take to get there?

12. How long was your school year?

13. What was a typical day like?

14. Can you recall the names of your teachers? What were they like?

15. Was anyone particularly helpful to you? Did any teacher give you a particularly hard time?

16. What courses do you remember taking? Were there any you liked? Any you disliked?

17. What kind of student were you?

18. Did you participate in any activities, sports, etc.? Play an instrument?

19. Who were your best friends?

20. Socially, were you popular? Shy?

21. What did you do for fun?

22. Did you learn to drive? If so, at what age? On what make of car? Stick or automatic transmission?

23. Did you graduate? If so, when? What was your graduation day like? Did you have a celebration?

24. What was your first job? Where did you work? What were your duties?

25. How much were you paid? What did you do with your money?

26. What did you do during summer vacation?

27. Did you attend any dances, formals, proms, etc.?

28. Did you receive any awards, honors, etc.?

29. As a teen, were you ever in trouble? If so, how did your parents handle it?

30. Did you enjoy your high school years?

31. If you could go back and relive your teen years, what would you do differently?

32. Did you have any rules that your parents enforced?

33. Did you date in high school? Who? What were your dates like?

34. Did you break up? If so, why?

35. What kind of music did you listen to?

36. Can you remember any popular slang terms from your teen years?

37. Can you remember any fads?

38. Was there any significant world event that impacted your high school years? (World War II, Korean War, etc.)

39. Did you have any favorite movie stars or heroes?

40. Any memorable teen or high school memory to include?

Personal History Questionnaire-5A

Young Adult/College

1. Did you attend college? (If not, skip to Questionnaire 5B.)

2. If you did, why did you decide to attend college?

3. What was the name of your college?

4. Where was it located?

5. Do you recall how much it cost to attend?

6. How did you meet those costs?

7. How many students attended your college?

8. What was your major?

9. Why did you choose that?

10. Did you have a minor?

11. Where did you live while attending?

12. Did you have a job while in school?

13. If so, what was it?

14. How much were you paid?

15. Did you have any favorite courses? Any that you detested?

16. Do you recall any of your professors?

17. Did you participate in any activities?

18. During what years did you attend this college?

19. Was there a professor, a counselor, etc., who particularly influenced you?

20. If you quit college, why did you quit?

21. How were your grades?

22. If you graduated, when did you graduate?

23. Do you have any special memories of college?

24. What was your school nickname? Your mascot? Your school colors? Your alma mater?

25. Do you have any memories of social activities?

26. Do you have any memories of sporting events?

27. Do you have any memories of your graduation day?

28. Did you receive any honors, awards, etc.?

29. What degree did you receive?

30. Did you attend graduate school?

31. If so, at which school?

32. When did you attend?

33. What did you concentrate in?

34. Where did you live while in grad school?

35. How did you pay your expenses while in grad school?

36. Did you receive a degree? If so, what was it?

37. Did you go on to any further education? If so, explain.

38. How do you think a college education affects a person's life?

39. If you have descendants, would you recommend they attend college?

40. Any special memory of your college days?

Personal History Questionnaire-5B

Young Adult/Military

(If you did not serve in the military, skip to Questionnaire 5C.)

1. If you served in the military, did you enlist or were you drafted?

2. When did you enter the service?

3. Where were you inducted?

4. How hard was it to leave home? How did you stay in touch with loved ones?

5. What rank were you when you joined? In which branch did you serve?

6. Were you inducted during a war?

7. If you enlisted, why did you join the service?

8. How was the adjustment from civilian life to military life?

9. What were you trained to do?

10. Where were you stationed? Were you stationed anywhere else? Where and for how long?

11. Did you ever see combat?

12. If so, describe the battles or campaigns in which you served?

13. Did you suffer any harm? What was your recovery like?

14. Were you afraid going into battle?

15. If so, how did you handle it?

16. Did you forge any special friendships while in the service?

17. Any reflections on your years of service?

18. If you served during a war, how do you view your former enemy now?

19. How do you view war now?

20. When did you leave the military?

21. At what rank where you mustered out?

22. Did you receive any medals, commendations, promotions, etc.?

23. Was it difficult readjusting to civilian life?

24. Do you think your service is appreciated by society?

25. Any special memory of your military years to include?

Personal History Questionnaire-5C

Young Adult/Early Career

1. After you left school, did you go to work?

2. If not, what did you do? (Skip to Q.15)

3. If you did take a job, for whom did you work?

4. How did you acquire the job?

5. Where was the company located?

6. Who was your first supervisor?

7. What were your responsibilities?

8. How long was your work day? Your work week?

9. Do you recall how much you were paid? Did you receive any benefits?

10. How did you get to work?

11. What did you wear to work? Uniforms?

12. Did you use any special equipment while performing your job?

13. Did you enjoy your work? Why or why not?

14. If you didn't enjoy your work, did you make plans to seek another position?

15. If you were still living at home, did you also have responsibilities there as well?

16. How long did you live at home?

17. If you did leave home, when was that?

18. Where did you live?

19. How did it feel to be independent?

20. As a young adult, did you have any dreams or plans for the future?

21. At that time of your life, what was the most important thing to you?

22. How did your family handle your new independence?

23. How did you spend your free time?

22. Any special memories of this time of life?

Questionnaire-6

Love and Marriage

1. How old were you when you first had thoughts of romance or were attracted to another?

2. Do you remember your first kiss?

3. Who was your first love?

4. Where did you meet him/her?

5. What do remember about your first love?

6. Do you recall any other significant loves or crushes?

7. What were the dating customs like then?

8. Did you marry? If so, when? (If married, skip to Q.10.) If not, how do you feel about that?

9. If never married, were you ever engaged? (If never engaged and never married, skip to Questionnaire 7. If ever engaged, skip to Q.12.)

10. Did you have any other serious relationships before your marriage?

11. Were you ever engaged prior to being engaged to your spouse? (If not, skip to Q.21 If yes, continue with Q.12.)

12. If engaged before, what was your fiancé's name?

13. How did you meet this person?

14. How long did you date this person before becoming engaged?

15. How did the engagement to this person occur?

16. Did you give or get an engagement ring to this person? What was it like? Do you remember how much it was worth?

17. How did your family react to your engagement?

18. How did your former fiancé's family react?

19. How long were you engaged before you broke up?

20. What caused the break up? How do you feel about that relationship now? (For those who never married, skip to Questionnaire 7. For those who married after a broken engagement, proceed to Q.21.)

21. How did you meet your mate?

22. Did you hit it off right way? Was it love at first sight?

23. When did you meet your mate?

24. What did you do while dating?

25. When did you realize that you were in love? How did you know you were in love?

26. When you became engaged, how did it happen?

27. Did you get or give a ring? What was it like, and do you remember how much it cost?

28. How did your family react to your engagement? How did your fiancé's family react?

29. How long were you engaged?

30. When you did get married, how did you choose your wedding date?

31. How did you plan your wedding?

32. Who helped with the planning?

33. Were there any showers or pre-wedding parties?

34. Where were you married?

35. Who officiated?

36. What kind of ceremony was it?

37. What was the weather like on that day?

38. Can you describe what you wore? Where did you obtain your wedding garments? Were there flowers?

39. Can you describe what your spouse wore?

40. How did you get to the wedding?

41. Who were your attendants? What did they wear? Did you give them any gifts?

42. What were your emotions on your wedding day? Were you nervous, happy, etc.?

43. Was there music? Do remember what was played?

44. Anything special that you remember from the ceremony?

45. How many guests attended?

46. Who do you remember attending?

47. Was there a reception or party afterward?

48. Where was it held? Was there food? A cake? Dancing? What did you dance to?

49. Is there anything that stands out in your memory about your reception?

50. Did you receive any noteworthy gifts?

51. Where did you spend your honeymoon?

52. How long was your honeymoon?

53. Anything you especially remember about your honeymoon?

54. Where did you live when you were first married?

55. Can you describe your first home?

56. What kind of furniture, appliances, etc. did you have?

57. How were your finances? Were things tight or wasn't money a concern?

58. Did you find adjusting to married life difficult?

59. How did you manage the household chores?

60. Did you have any pets? If so, the name and what kind of animal.?

61. Did you quarrel as newlyweds?

62. How did you resolve your quarrels?

63. What do you think attracted your spouse to you?

64. Why do you think your spouse fell in love with you?

65. What did you find most attractive about your spouse?

66. Why do you think you fell in love with your spouse?

67. What did you admire most about your spouse?

68. How long did that marriage last?

69. Did you face any serious hardships during your early years of marriage?

70. Do you have any advice for newlyweds?

71. Do you have any special memories of your newlywed days?

Questionnaire-6A

Divorce, Remarriage, and Death of a Spouse

(If never divorced, widowed, or remarried, skip to Questionnaire 7.)

1. Were you ever divorced? (If divorced, go to Q.3.)

2. Have you ever lost a spouse to death? (If widowed, skip to Q.40.)

3. If divorced, what were the circumstances?

4. How did you handle this disappointment?

5. How did your family and society view your divorce?

6. Were there children involved? How was custody arranged?

7. How did the divorce affect your children?

8. How did you handle your new status? Did you need to take a job? Move to another home, etc.?

9. Is there anything you regret about your failed marriage?

10. After you divorced, did you ever think you would remarry?

11. Did you remarry? If yes, on what date? (If yes, continue with Q.12. If no, skip to Questionnaire 7.)

12. If you did remarry, where did you meet your second spouse?

13. How long after did you meet your new spouse?

14. Were you hesitant or eager to become involved again?

15. How was it to date again?

16. When did you know you were in love?

17. When did you become engaged?

18. How did you become engaged?

19. Was your attitude any different when approaching this new marriage?

20. When were you married?

21. Where were you married?

22. Was this wedding less elaborate than your first wedding?

23. What did you wear?

24. What did your spouse wear?

25. What did your attendants wear?

26. If you had children from your previous marriage, how did this affect your decision to marry again?

27. If you had children, how did you blend your new family?

28. Did your new spouse have children?

29. If so, how did you get along with your stepchildren?

30. Was there a reception after your wedding?

31. How many guests attended? What was the reception like?

32. Did you receive gifts?

33. Did you go on a honeymoon?

34. Where did you live after your remarriage?

35. Did you find it difficult to be married again?

36. Did you find it difficult to refrain from comparing your new spouse to your former one?

37. How long did this marriage last?

38. Were there any hardships that you had to face in this marriage?

39. Were there any subsequent divorces or remarriages? (If so, repeat Q.1 –Q.39. If no, skip to Questionnaire 7.)

40. If your spouse died, what were the circumstances of the death?

41. On what date did your spouse die?

42. What do you remember most about your partner's death?

43. How did you handle the grief? How long did you mourn?

44. How did you handle being single again?

45. Did your spouse's death impact you financially? If so, what changes did you have to make?

46. If you had children, were they small or grown when their parent passed away?

47. How did you help them to cope?

48. What is your fondest memory of your deceased spouse?

49. What advice would you offer to anyone suffering through the death of a spouse?

50. Did you remarry after the death of your spouse? (If no, go to Questionnaire 7. If yes, proceed to Q.12 and answer Q.12 through Q.40.)

Questionnaire-7

Birth of Children

1. Did you have children? If not, how do you feel about that? (If no children, skip ahead to Questionnaire 8.)

2. Did you ever have any struggles with infertility?

3. How did you handle that difficulty?

4. When you dreamed of having children, how many did you hope to have in the beginning? How many boys? How many girls?

5. What kind of parent did you hope to be before you became one? Do you think you lived up to your ideal?

6. When did you suspect that your first child was on its way?

7. How did you find out about the pregnancy?

8. How did you feel knowing you would soon be a parent?

9. How did your family and your spouse's family react?

10. Did you (or your wife) go to a doctor right away? Who was that doctor?

11. Were there any pregnancy complications?

12. What kind of pre-natal treatment was there at the time?

13. How did you prepare for the baby's arrival? How did your spouse? Did you set up a nursery? Buy clothes? Was there a shower?

14. Did you (or your wife) have to give up a job because of the pregnancy?

15. If so, how did this affect your family finances?

16. Where was your first baby born?

17. Was the birth at home or in a hospital? What preparations were made? Who attended the birth?

18. Was the delivery difficult or easy? How long was the labor?

19. Were there any complications during the delivery? How was pain handled?

20. What was the cost of delivering the baby?

21. Was the baby a boy or girl?

22. When was the baby born? Date? Time?

23. What did you name the baby? How did you arrive at that name?

24. How much did the baby weigh and how long was it?

25. What were your feelings when you first saw your baby?

26. What or who did the baby look like?

27. How long was your (or your wife's) convalescence?

28. What changes did the baby bring to the household?

29. What was the baby's personality? Colicky? A good sleeper?

30. How was your baby's health?

31. What did you most enjoy about being a parent?

32. What surprised you most about parenthood?

33. Any specials memories of your first child?

34. Did you have another child? (If no, skip to Questionnaire 7A. If yes, proceed to Q.35.)

35. How was that pregnancy/delivery different?

36. What did you have a boy or a girl?

37. What is this child's birthday? Where was it born?

38. What did you name the baby? Why did you name it that?

39. How much did this baby weigh and how long was it?

40. What did the baby look like? What was its personality?

41. How did you feel upon this child's arrival?

42. What special memories did you have of your second/subsequent child/children?

43. Did you have any more children? (If yes, for each child go back to Q34 and repeat for each subsequent pregnancy.)

44. Have you ever lost a pregnancy or a child/children? If so, what were the circumstances? How did you cope with such a loss?

Questionnaire-7A

Family Life

1. Did you move to a larger home as your family grew? If so, where did you move and for how long did you live at each place?

2. How did you and your spouse provide for your children?

3. What were your children like when they were small?

4. Did they get along with each other?

5. How did you manage sibling rivalry?

6. In what style of clothing did you dress your children? How was their hair styled?

7. What kind of games, pastimes did your children enjoy?

8. Did you have any pets? If yes, what kind of animals? What were their names?

9. Did you take your children on outings, sporting events, or vacations?

10. Can you recall a time when your child or children embarrassed you?

11. Can you recall a time when you embarrassed them?

12. Were your children healthy? If not, how so?

13. Did you have any home remedies?

14. Where did your children attend school?

15. Were you involved at their school or in their activities?

16. How did you celebrate your children's birthdays?

17. What holidays did you celebrate? How did you celebrate them?

18. How did you handle discipline? Did you spank them?

19. What kind of worries did you have for them?

20. What were their natural inclinations or talents?

21. Were there any family rules?

22. Did you share a family faith? If so, where did you worship?

23. Can you recall any significant religious occasions that your children celebrated i.e. baptism, first communion, bar mitzvah, etc.?

24. Can you recall any hardships that affected your family life?

25. Were there any historical events that affected your family life, i.e. The Depression, war, etc.?

26. From whom did you seek advice on how to raise children?

27. What was the best advice that you received? What was the worst?

28. Did you ever find it difficult to balance your needs with those of your family?

29. Any special memories of family life?

30. How did your children change when they entered their teen years?

31. Did those years present any special challenges? How did you handle them?

32. When did each child leave home? How did you feel at the time?

33. Is there anything you would do differently in how you raised your children?

34. What advice would you give to parents today?

35. Do you think it more difficult to raise children today?

36. Are you a grandparent?

37. If so, how many grandchildren do you have?

38. What is the name and birth date of your first/next grandchild?

39. How did you feel when you learned you were going to be a grandparent?

40. When you saw this grandchild, what did you think?

41. Can you recall how you felt about this grandchild?

42. Do you have more than one grandchild? (If yes, for each grandchild repeat Q38 –41.)

43. What was your style of grandparenting?

44. How does being a grandparent differ from being a parent?

45. Are you a great-grandparent?

46. If so, how many great-grandchildren do you have? (If yes, for each great-grandchild repeat Q47–48.)

47. What is the name and birth date of this great-grandchild?

48. When you saw this great-grandchild, what did you think? Feel?

49. How does being a great-grandparent differ from being a grandparent? From being a parent?

Personal History Questionnaire-8

Middle Age & Empty Nest

(If you have no children, skip to Q.9.)

1. How did you adjust to your grown children's independence?

2. Was it difficult adjusting to having an "empty nest"?

3. If your children married, when did each get married and to whom did they marry?

4. How did you feel on each of their wedding days?

5. How did you view your role as an in-law?

6. After the children were grown, did you begin any special endeavors?

7. How did you support your grown children and remain connected to them?

8. If you were still married, how did your relationship change after the children were gone?

9. Do you believe in mid-life crisis?

10. Were there any noteworthy physical changes that occurred during your middle years? When did you develop gray hair, etc.?

11. Did it bother you to see signs of aging?

12. At that time, what was your attitude regarding aging?

13. Now that you are older, how has your attitude changed?

14. At what age do you think a person is truly old?

15. During middle age, many people begin to experience loss or have already experienced the loss either of loved ones, of dreams, friends, etc. How did you handle any such losses?

16. How was your health during your middle years?

17. At what time in your life would you consider yourself to have been at your prime?

18. Any special memories of your middle years?

Questionnaire-9

Earning a Living

1. What has been your main job, career or method of earning a living? (If you ever owned a business, answer Questionnaire9A too.)

2. Did you have any other jobs before beginning your main career?

3. If yes, how many? (For each job answer Q. 4-12)

4. What was the nature of the job?

5. Where was the job located?

6. When did you work there?

7. How did you acquire that position?

8. What were your duties, responsibilities?

9. How much were you paid?

10. What did you think of that job?

11. What prompted you to leave that job?

12. What was your next job?

13. Why did you take the job where you spent most of your career?

14. What made you stay and make it your life's work?

15. How many years were you in your main job?

16. Do you remember your starting salary?

17. Did your position change over the years?

18. Has your employer changed over time?

19. Has the tools or technology associated with your work changed since you first began?

20. What was a typical workday like for you?

21. Did you ever have a low point during your career?

22. If so, what was it and how did you handle it?

23. Did you ever have any high points?

24. If so, what was it and how did it affect you?

25. Did you enjoy your career?

26. Did you ever travel for your job? If yes, where?

27. Did you ever attend special training or receive special education for this career?

28. Were you ever laid-off? Terminated? How did you handle that?

29. What do you consider the main accomplishments of your working life?

30. Did you ever find it difficult to balance work with personal life?

31. Looking back, what are the most valuable things you learned from working?

32. Did you retire from your main career?

33. If retired, when did you begin to think about retiring?

34. When you were young, when did people stop working?

35. What did you hope to do when you retired? Did you have any dreams?

36. What considerations did you keep in mind in making your decision to retire?

37. When did you actually retire?

38. Did you have any celebration when you ceased working?

39. Was retirement like you thought it would be?

40. How did you adjust to this new stage of life?

41. If you lived with another person, how did they cope with your new stage of life?

42. Has anything been especially difficult for you since retiring?

43. How has the change in financial status affected your life?

44. How has your health been?

45. If you have suffered with poor health, how did you deal with this misfortune?

46. If you are in good health, how do you maintain your physical condition?

47. What did you do with your extra time?

48. Did you belong to any social, religious, volunteer groups, etc.?

49. What advice would you give to your descendants regarding health?

50. What advice would you give them about preparing for retirement with regards to finances?

51. Do you think the retirement years are truly the golden years?

52. What do you look forward to in the coming years?

Questionaire-9A

Owning a Business

1. Have you ever owned your own business or have you ever been self-employed?

2. If so, what was the name of your business?

3. What was the nature of the business?

4. Did you have a business partner? If so, how did your relationship develop? Did you maintain a good business relationship?

5. Was starting a business always a dream of yours?

6. How much preparation went into the startup of the business?

7. When you began, how much money did you invest in it?

8. How many hours a week did you work at it?

9. When did your business become profitable, if ever?

10. Would you consider your business a successful one?

11. If so, how did your business grow and expand?

12. Did you enjoy owning your own business?

13. What was the outcome of the business?

14. Would you recommend that others go into business for themselves?

15. What lessons did you learn from operating your own company?

Questionnaire-10

All About You

1. Do you have any special talents, skills, gifts?

2. If so, how do you express them?

3. Have you ever traveled any place memorable?

4. Have you developed any special relationships or friendships during your lifetime? If so, how did you meet that person and what was the nature of your relationship?

5. Have you ever belonged to any civic organizations? Political organizations? Service organizations? Religious organizations?

6. Have you had any hobbies?

7. Has religion or faith played a role in your life?

8. What do you think is your most admirable quality?

9. What do you think is your least admirable quality?

10. What are you most proud of in your life?

11. If you could go back and change anything about your life, what would it be?

12. What was the most difficult time of your life?

13. What was the best time of your life?

14. Who has been the greatest influence on your life?

15. Do you admire anyone. If yes, who? And why?

16. Do you have a favorite sports team? Song? Movie? Book? Television show? What did you like about them?

17. Did you have a favorite movie star? Athlete? Singer? Writer? Artist?

18. Did you have a personal motto that you lived by? If so, what is it and how did you come to adopt it?

19. Have you ever experienced a miracle or an amazing coincidence?

20. What has it been like to grow old?

21. What do you value most in life?

22. What is the nicest thing anyone has ever said to you?

23. What is the nicest thing anyone has ever done for you?

24. What is the best thing you ever did for someone else?

25. What is the most embarrassing thing that has ever happened to you?

26. What is the funniest thing that has ever happened to you?

27. Do you have a philosophy for living your life?

28. Do you have any advice for young people or your descendants?

29. Were you politically active? What was your political party or political philosophy?

30. How would you like to be remembered?

Questionnaire-11

Your World

1. Do you have any recollections of The Depression?

2. Any recollections of Prohibition?

3. Do you have any memories of Pearl Harbor? World War II?

4. The end of World War II?

5. The Korean War?

6. The Kennedy Assassination?

7. The Vietnam War and the turbulent Sixties?

8. The Moon Landing?

9. The terrorist attacks of September 11, 2001

10. Is there any other historical event that you particularly remember?

11. Is there any historical figure that you admired or particularly remember?

12. Many things have changed during your lifetime. Compare your life today to when you were younger.

13. How have homes and family life changed during your lifetime?

14. What do you feel is the greatest invention for the home? Indoor plumbing? Electricity? Dishwashers, etc.?

15. How has transportation changed during your lifetime?

16. How has medicine changed?

17. How has technology changed?

18. How have the roles of women and men changed? Do you think that those roles have changed for the better or worse?

19. How has the country's economic situation changed?

20. How has society changed? Do you think it has changed for the better or worse?

21. What do you think is the most significant historical event of your lifetime?

Questionnaire-12

Wild Card Questions

1. I was furious when . . .

2. I hate to brag, but I'm very good at . . .

3. It was so out of character for me when I . . .

4. I cried so hard when . . .

5. I wonder why . . .

6. I couldn't believe it when . . .

7. I admit I was jealous when . . .

8. Looking back, I still can't believe I ever . . .

9. I was terrified when . . .

10. I never did understand why . . .

11. One thing I've learned is . . .

12. I laughed hysterically when . . .

13. I was very selfless when I . . .

14. One thing I'll never do is . . .

15. I was in way over my head when . . .

16. I had a heavy heart the day I . . .

17. I'll always regret that . . .

18. You'd never know it, but I . . .

19. I was never more relieved than when . . .

20. I got the biggest thrill when . . ..

A Final Word

Many things can come between your desire to record your life story and actually completing it.

If you find that you are having difficulty achieving your goal, Gleamings Personal Historian Services, can help. We can coach you through the process, take what you have already written and edit it, or create a complete personal history for you.

In addition, we offer other services such as institutional histories; military histories; memorial books; ethical wills; pet memorials; birthday, wedding, anniversary, and reunion histories; etc. If you have a memory, we can preserve it.

We also offer workshops where we teach your group how to write their life story.

For more information, contact:

Gleamings Personal Historian Services

Janicelanepalko@gmail.com

Your life is our business!

www.ingramcontent.com/pod-product-compliance
Lightning Source LLC
Chambersburg PA
CBHW060514280326
41933CB00014B/2962
* 9 7 8 0 9 9 8 4 2 9 6 0 1 *